IN DEFENSE
OF
SENIORHOOD

Riya Aarini

In Defense of Seniorhood

Text copyright © 2022 by Riya Aarini

This is a work of fiction. Names, characters, businesses, places, events, locales, and incidents are either the products of the author's imagination or used in a fictitious manner. Any resemblance to actual persons, living or dead, or actual events is purely coincidental.

ISBN: 978-1-956496-09-3 (Paperback)

ISBN: 978-1-956496-10-9 (eBook)

Library of Congress Control Number: 2022916457

First published in Austin, Texas, USA

Visit www.riyapresents.com

CONTENTS

CONTENTS

ON REALIZING I WAS A SENIOR

I didn't fully grasp that I was a senior until a few uncannily similar life experiences began to snowball. I first took notice when the casino no longer asked for my ID. I casually assumed it was because I was a familiar, friendly face. Beers were delivered from the local pizza chain without the delivery gal requesting my ID at the front door. I figured, "It's only a pizza and beer; they must be lax." Soon enough, young men and women would punctuate every answer, statement, or question with "Sir." I was tickled by their sincere show of respect. The polite ones would hold the door open for me and smile tenderly, like I was someone's grandpa. I entertained the notion that it was simply due to my looking distinguished and important. The big shocker came when I found myself paying keen attention to life insurance commercials, and a flood of mail consisting of invitations to join the national association for retired folks started pouring in. I began to shudder at the thought of slipping on icy sidewalks, cringe at the prospect of walking up the stairs, and refuse the option of driving at night. After experiencing all these peculiarities, I developed the nagging suspicion that I had reached what society officially deems to be a mature age. Once again, people began to ask for my ID everywhere I went. For a few exhilarating moments, I was on top of the world, feeling like all the good folks mistook me for a lithe twenty-five-year-old again—until I realized that they were simply following protocol to verify my age for my senior citizen discount.

ON BS DETECTORS

Listen, since I've made it to old age, it means only one thing: I'm smart enough to have achieved this rare milestone. Not everyone does. I've used enough brainpower over the last several decades to circumvent the crooks, dodge the scandals, and avoid all the nonsense from folks who make life unnecessarily unpleasant. Old age is not for the faint of heart or weak in mind. Laziness, corruption, and an endless sea of stupidity surround us like humpback whale pods circling schools of sardines. It takes a well-oiled BS detector, a magnanimous spirit, and a generous dose of luck to reach an age as venerable as mine. Not only

3

that, but you'll need to follow your gut instincts in order to survive the constant rigors of this planet. When you come face to face with the malarkey, hear nothing but baloney, or are fed excuses that fail to pass the sniff test, you just might want to call them out on it. And our extensive unintended life experience in the company of fools makes it easier to say exactly what's on our minds.

ON SENIOR DISCOUNTS

If there's anything that makes aging worth all the effort, it's the senior citizen discount. I've waited seventy-plus years to be able to take 10 percent off almost everything, a perk I proudly share with six living US presidents. Thanks to my senior discount, I enjoy free coffee every morning with the guys at the local fast-food joint. It's a real bonding experience. Then I take the missus out for an evening of fine dining at the lobster house—made possible by presenting my senior card. With our discount, we book four-day cruises to the South Pacific just to keep up our zest for life. I tag along with the missus to shop for my Hawaiian floral shirts on Wednesdays; and as I open my wallet, I never forget to bring up my senior discount to the friendly cashier. There's nothing that beats the joy in being treated extra special just for reaching a financially life-changing milestone. After all, when you get to be my age, there's hardly anything else on earth that delivers such satisfaction—except for the grandkids. It's as if society gives you a grateful nod for simply occupying the planet for almost three-quarters of a century. Anyhow, after contributing seventy-some years of spending power to a world of inflation, shrinkflation, and recessions, I've definitely earned my senior citizen discount.

ON HEARING

I may ask "What?" a few times before answering your question, but mind you, I've grown to have supersensitive hearing, kind of like Supersenior. So when that upstairs neighbor walks across the floor, it sounds to me like the angels in heaven are having a grand old time bowling and striking way more often than I'd like to hear or that massive clouds of roaring thunder are ominously rolling our way or that the mountains are rumbling with all the fury of a four-engine aircraft jet upon takeoff. What sounds like a tiny squeak to you actually sounds like a thousand galloping horses to me. So be gentle and repeat yourself when

I ask. Yelling your answer, by the way, won't do either of us any good. You'll grow hoarse, and I'll interpret you raising your voice as a fit of anger. An aging person doesn't need to hear hee-haws every time a simple question gets asked. I just might not ask you questions anymore. How'd you like that? Oh, wait, pretend I didn't ask.

ON EVERYONE PASSING

Everyone's dying, dropping like flies. What the heck? I often have to ask myself, "What's in the fruit punch?" Almost every day I read the obituaries to find a name I recognize or hear about through a casual phone call. Talking about a friend's passing is normally done without all the fanfare, agony, or disbelief typical of our youth. Rather, we talk about it as nonchalantly as we discuss the weather. That's how accustomed to it we are: rain today, snow tomorrow, Harold yesterday, Janice last week. When I make the count, I find most of my friends are dead instead of alive. It gets to be a weekly thing now, me and my happy-to-be-alive buddies chatting about who unexpectedly sped off on the four-lane highway to heaven. Even the expected partings are a shocker, being just another in-your-face reminder of the inevitable closing in. I guess once you've attained senior status, no one's death is truly an untimely surprise. It might be that soon enough, I'll be the only one left hobbling in my social circle. Once you reach my age, you just have to wonder who's going to be around tomorrow. No kidding, even today's a gamble.

ON CHANGING THE WORLD

O nce the sense got knocked into me in old age, I gave up pursuing the illusion that I can change the world. As illusions go, they're just not realistically solvable. Even if I play a small part in fixing one world crisis, there's always another to deal with right around the bend. It's a cycle that goes on ad infinitum. See, world problems are like the annoying drip in a dripping faucet—there's always another drop ready to fall. I've learned to take a step back and focus on solving the more pressing issues, like the carton of milk not opening up properly or that freaky centipede infestation behind the toilet or not being able to fit my hand into a circular can of sour-cream-and-onion potato chips. I'm busy enough trying to deal with the toothpaste falling off my toothbrush and still being unable to figure out what all those switches on the wall turn on. So don't bother me with pleas to try to change the world. I've got more important things to worry about.

ON BEING IRRELEVANT

As I climb the weather-resistant aluminum ladder of age, the folks still on the bottom rungs have the nerve to treat me like I'm irrelevant. It's like with every birthday in recent years, I become more and more invisible. In fact, in the eyes and ears of youth, we seniors are as useless as the landline phone, gone to the wayside and buried alongside its partner, the once-extraordinary pay phone—which, at its zenith, was unhesitatingly used even by caped superheroes. Gray-haired and arthritic, I'm treated like obsolete print newspapers and—considered equally atrocious—paper maps. Millennials feel just as confident reading paper maps as I do digital ones. I'm as relevant to today's generations as the fax machine screeching like a red-tailed hawk warning other raptors to back off. I'm hoping I won't have the same fate as parking meters that have been turned into street art. Trying to paint me pretty can only go so far. Even though I'm a walking encyclopedia of world knowledge, facts, and figures, I'm deemed as archaic as those bulky twenty-two-volume sets. And when it comes to the internet, don't waste your time asking Google, because I probably know better. Now listen, I refuse to be defined by my age. In all honesty, we seniors consider up-and-coming hot shots brimming with more bravado and reckless abandon than knowledge and experience to be just as irrelevant. So all in all, it's fair.

ON STEREOTYPES

You know, when I was young, I had the studly musculature of a jackhammer construction worker. Now, I'm wrinkly and plain. In my youth I was bold, daring, and brave enough to speak my mind. Today, I'm blunt. Back in my handsome heyday, I was known as a hot ticket, exciting, and risqué. Nowadays, I'm a gray-headed, overly amorous senior citizen with an annoying habit of laying on the compliments a little too heavy. Nothing's changed about me except for the fact that I've got a few more decades behind me. What gives? I'll tell you what: it's the age factor that changes everything. I've been relegated to an awful stereotype,

15

one that needs to be broken like the laws of physics, or walnuts, or the record for the fastest time to unravel a roll of toilet paper with one hand. All I'm asking for is a positive, open-minded conversation, where you might stand to gain some wisdom from speaking to someone who's been around a while. In the meantime, I'll surround myself with the younger generations and stay engaged with the world—as a plain, blunt, and overly passionate senior citizen.

ON SLOWING DOWN

Listen, I've learned to take my time with everything I do these days. Don't get me wrong. When I was a young stud, speed was my name, and fast was my game. I was faster than a bolt of lightning, faster than a cheetah at the safari park, faster than a fast-talker tricks you into participating in a modern-day Ponzi scheme. So I know a thing or two about speed. Nowadays, though, I've slowed down. I stop and smell the roses, take a few minutes each morning to watch the sun rise, and actually pause to listen more carefully to all the presumptuous spiels the youngsters spill. Now, if you find me slow, you're in the wrong lane, buddy.

Accelerate out of the slow lane and into the fast lane where you belong. See, I've already spent my heyday being proud of my over one hundred speedometer readings. Now I'm all set to enjoy the days I have left, in stride, and in my own designated lane. Actually, roadside flowers do tend to bloom off the side of the slow lane, and, for once in my life, I'm grateful to stop and smell them. You just might shift gears, too, when you start to run out of gas. Take it from me, kiddo: the roadside flowers will always be there, so you, too, can stop to smell them anytime.

ON ADULT DIAPERS

If there's one thing I've got in common with the grandkids, it's the godsent diaper. While they preserve my dignity, I wouldn't yell to the world that I've got a pair on. See, astonishingly, babies pull off wearing the diaper with characteristic ease. Rather than be embarrassed by wearing their cushiony disposable diapers, babies wear the absorbent chunks of petroleum-derived plastic with signature pride, as if their generously covered rump is all a part of their natural cuteness factor. I can't help but to humbly ask, what changes from age zero to age seventy-two? Incomprehensible as it is to younger folks, I don't mind wearing pull-ups everywhere I go: on afternoon shopping excursions, to the beach, and on long-distance hikes along the scenic trails. I argue that it's far more embarrassing to have an accident than it is to wear a comfortable form of adult protection. After all, a weak bladder was never on my bucket list. But being able to hike the canyons without an accident was—and the pull-ups helped me cross that glorious experience off my list. I've been there and done that—thanks to my adult pull-ups. Anyway, since I've said a firm no to the horrific passing trend of wearing emasculating skinny jeans, donning a discreet form of incontinence protection isn't a kick in the seat of my pants. Remember, just because I'm hiking the last section on the stunning long-distance trail of life, it doesn't mean I have to give up my pride.

ON TECHNOLOGY

I've lived on this earth for nearly three-quarters of a century, so I've seen it all. That is, until technology invited itself in and changed everything I know in an instant. It's like starting from scratch, as if my seventy-plus years of existence meant nothing. Upon attempting to operate one of the latest devices, I end up red in the face, boiling like an egg, simmering like a pot of chili, and frying like a fillet of Alaskan cod. By the time I painstakingly learn to operate the device, they release a brand-new one, and I have the unwanted trouble of relearning everything. I'm over seventy years old—I don't have that kind of time. Clearly, my frustrations are valid. See, I had the whole world sized up. I knew how everything worked before technology arrived. People asked *me* all the questions. Now that technology has become mainstream, I find myself asking every twenty-year-old the silliest of questions about it. It's role reversal at its finest. Seems like nothing can be accomplished without technology interfering. I am somewhat comforted that tech companies considerately think of us gramps and market senior-friendly gadgets, like smartphones with extra-large numbers. But I just end up feeling as powerless as my grandkids, who fiddle with their own emoji phones with extra-large numbers. It's a little patronizing and accommodating at the same time. I admit I've adapted somewhat. The only tech gadget I find both useful and operable is an automatic jar opener. I need my beans. So quit piling the latest technology on my plate. It's already piled high with three-bean salad. Now, excuse me while I peacefully eat my salad *without* a phone attached to my side.

ON FIRSTS

You may view me as silver haired, wrinkled, and hard of hearing. Nothing impressive, right? Though I no longer boast of youth, I'm privileged to have been around for some of the world's finest firsts and live to tell you about them. Over an existence that's spanned a majestic seventy-plus-year timeline, I've been witness to the famous Apollo 13 mission, the third attempt to land on the moon. I was just an overenthusiastic youth glued to the color television when that crucial phrase, "Houston, we've had a problem," entered mainstream movies, song lyrics, and even today's popular culture. Believe me when I say I'm as old as email itself, when hearing the perky voice chirping, "You've got mail!" justified a small-scale celebration. You may think chat rooms are relatively new to the party, but the first videotape recorder was born when yours truly was in diapers—ahem, baby diapers, that is. I've inserted one of the first floppy disks, complete with a remarkable 80 KB storage capacity. My early years coincided with the invention of the first pocket calculator, which, in today's dollars, cost two-and-a-half-thousand to call it yours and tuck inside a front shirt pocket along with a plastic pocket protector bursting with half a dozen ballpoint ink pens. And finally, a personal first I proudly observed was our very own twenty-sixth Constitutional Amendment, which gave eighteen-year-olds the right to vote. Yeah, I'm amazed myself at the contributions I've seen made to humankind. Witnessing these events makes me feel like I was a part of them. And I was. So under this head of silvery hair and ears that don't hear so well is a lifetime of unrepeatable firsts.

ON BEING GRUMPY

All right, I can be grumpy. But I've got reasons—
and good ones. See, I've had hopes and dreams
from my youth dashed into pieces, gone up in smoke,
disappear into the neverlands of never ever, not in this
lifetime, pal. I'm a ball of chronic pain. Not even an
extra-strength aspirin is strong enough to take away the
aches that never fail to surprise me, like smiling quokkas
or funeral mimes. Most of my lifelong friends are
gone—and they're perfect reminders of what'll happen
to me next. So my grumpy attitude is perfectly valid.
I'll let you in on a secret known only to the intimate
world of seniors: we realize we can get away scot-free

with being unnecessarily grumpy whenever we please. Young folks patronizingly dismiss our dramatic foibles, attributing them to old age. Heh! It gives us all the more reason to make a wild show of our grumpiness. I can be unhesitatingly blunt without taking an extra fifteen minutes to dig for exactly the right word that would make my comments more palatable. In that sense, I'm like a mischievous two-year-old who knows he can escape the consequences of anything—even a display of the grand old grumps. Plus, given the extent of my life experience, I'm less tolerant of baloney—and salami and pastrami. So think twice before you try to pull a fast one on a worldly-wise senior. Considering I've seen it all, few things excite me, challenge me in a meaningful way, or stump me—except technology, which has the opposite effect and frustrates me. Also, try opening a jar sometime.

ON GRAVESTONE INSCRIPTIONS

I have a grand time cemetery hopping and chuckling at gravestone inscriptions. It's a new pastime I can't put down. Gravestones are something I will eventually relate to, and I reckon I have to start planning if I want to make it out with a bang. Now, I don't want the usual stuff, like "Here lies a great father." I already know, as I've surprisingly raised three happy daughters with only one bathroom in the house. I don't need to hear that I've been a great husband. I've already arranged for flowers to be delivered to my wife on our anniversary every year after my death. "He was a good friend" is not news to me, as I've bought countless rounds of beer for the guys in my day. Simply put, I don't want to forever rest in peace knowing what I already know. Rather, I'd like something I've never known about myself or my life inscribed on my gravestone, something that'll keep me rolling all eternity or something I can joke about with the other angels. In all solemnity, however, "The wifey had an affair with Lou, and here lies the hubby who never knew" is not one of them.

ON LIFE BEING A GAMBLE

You don't get the privilege of being my age by playing your cards all wrong. Indeed, life is a gamble—but not like a game of blackjack, where your game is against the dealer. Rather, it's more like a game of poker, where your game is against the other players. And these other players just might try to do you in. So as in life, learn about what works—basically, the winning poker hands. Don't look inexperienced. Refrain from gambling more than you're willing to lose. Make it a point to play your opponents more than playing your cards. Instincts are everything in poker, as in life, and you stand to improve your strategy when you develop quick ones. Avoid acting out of turn, and never make a show of what you're about to do before you do it. Learn the strategies of poker in order to apply them to life, and it's my bet that you'll be just fine, making it up to my age, at the very least. If you have a good hand, by all means, raise the bet. Just remember, with a little bit of well-timed luck, even the worst hand can win the game.

ON DASHED DREAMS

Along with age comes the promise of the unfulfilled dream of youth. It's almost a guarantee of growing older. It's not even a money-back guarantee, and that alone should be downright illegal. Equally terrible is that the personal and financial investments we made in trying to make those priceless dreams a reality go shamefully unreturned. It's nothing short of an elder scam committed by Destiny, leaving most seniors who've ever dared to dream with a sour taste in their mouths and the sting of bitterness well into old age. We get to dwell on our life failures during the empty mornings of our retirement, our bedridden afternoons, and the final hurrahs of our last days. Destiny sure has its way of toying with the older folks. And the young'uns call us grumpy for no reason. Hmph!

ON STILL TRYING TO FIGURE IT OUT

Considering my increasingly gray hair and the fact that I take an entire minute to ponder your question before finally giving you a hesitant but astute answer, I may come across as incredibly wise—but I'm still trying to figure it out. While I've got youth and middle age fairly nailed, old age brings with it an entirely new set of situations and complications. I'm dealing with chronic pains I've never had before and adult children who rarely visit (which can be a good thing in some cases), not to mention financial setbacks and the potential fall of Social Security in this glorious time and age. All these frustrations take the spark out of my senior years. Just like the toddler wonders out loud what to do, as an aging person, I ask myself that same question every day. I've never grown out of it. Seriously, it doesn't get old, despite me getting to be so. In spite of gaining all this hard-earned life experience and wisdom, I still haven't even come close to figuring it all out. I'm starting to think it was never intended to work that way. Life is meant to be a conundrum from the beginning to the end. It's like an unsolvable Sudoku puzzle. Logic will only get me so far, making it necessary to add an element of guessing to the whole game of life thing. And we all know how terrible guessing can be. Ever try guessing how much salt to add to the soup? Or a woman's age? Or who let one rip in a crowded elevator?

ON NOT TAKING IT WITH YOU

If I've picked up anything in life—and I've never been one to leave a lonely penny lying on the ground—it's that building relationships is far more gratifying than building bank accounts. Now, I might live on a meager fixed income, and I might have looming medical bills to pay, and I might live well beyond my savings, but I'm astonishingly content. See, I've come to know that you can't take any of it with you. That's right: no matter how many physical possessions I accumulate, from my antique rustic hand-carved armoire to my fishing boat I fondly christened *Penelope*, nothing's coming with me when I make my final exit. They won't even fit through the door, much less make it past the pearly gates with its limiting twelve-foot diameter. I wouldn't want to be remembered as the one whose oversize furniture accidentally put a nick on the finials of the heavenly gates. But relationships, now that's a different story. The love of friends, spouses, and grandkids comes with me when I take off. They're just a part of me like nothing else. So take it from the experienced folks who've learned a little too late that working our breeches off was not worth the trouble and that all those lost opportunities for conversations, cuddles, and time spent together on make-your-own-pizza night will be sorely missed.

ON LONELINESS

"Get a social life." Now that's a remark coming from someone who doesn't need to excuse himself four or five times after sipping a medium soda during a movie matinee at the local theater. It makes trying to stay engrossed in a film a heightened ordeal. A few of us prefer to stay at home anyway. Despite the lonesome evenings, don't interrupt me watching my favorite serialized mystery TV show, because, to a senior who's fully invested in figuring out the scumbag whodunnit, your arbitrary and well-meaning distraction will be an epic fail. On occasion, I do hit the senior center to liven up the days, rhythmically shuffling my feet on its dance floor or playing bingo while vying for the grand prize of an artificial petunia arrangement that'll literally endure forever. Ironically, what all the hoopla of a random day out amounts to is an irreplaceable feeling of contentment to be back home, slipping into my pajamas, swallowing my benzodiazepines, and collapsing into bed. It's a senior's ideal way to combat loneliness when there's little else to fill the void: no work, no kids, nothing but the dreary companionship of isolation and financial stresses—undesirable friends, to say the least. Speaking of friends, at one low point, my dearest friend was the bubbly gal who filled my weekly pastrami order at the supermarket deli counter. I wised up and reconnected with my old pals, who are now my hobby buddies. I have what I consider to be a full social life again. It's not so bad. I mean, it's a leg up from the cliques of twentysomething-year-old friends who hit the bar and, instead of participating in titillating conversations, remain unflinchingly engrossed in their phones the whole evening. And you thought I was lonely.

ON WAITING

Time is a luxury I don't have. That's right, as an irreversibly aging senior, my time is limited. I've only got so much of it left on earth, and it's uncomfortably unpredictable. So I make it a point to avoid waiting whenever I reasonably can. See, I don't have time to wait in line for a creamy cup of a distinctly layered cappuccino. How many seniors have you seen patiently waiting in the exceedingly long lines at the corner coffee shop? There's a reason for that. We honestly don't know if we'll be around long enough to make it to the front of the line to place our order and have a sip of the carefully crafted caffeinated beverage.

I avoid waiting for busy elevators in twenty-story high-rise buildings for similar reasons. I rarely preorder a book, not sure if I'll be there to peruse its pages when it's finally released months later. At my age, I don't count on having the time to wait for green bananas to ripen yellow, either. As a matter of common sense, I don't even buy them anymore.

ON BEING STUBBORN

I may be stubborn as a mule to you. But mind you, mules are stubborn because they possess an abundance of common sense, which is akin to a natural form of genius. That strong sense of self-preservation gained after being in a world of endless nonsense has gotten me to the age I am today. So I'm inclined to resist anything that fails to pass the sniff test—and there's loads of steaming crap sitting in the fields. I'm also consistently right. Like the stubborn mule, I've seen quite a number of fences in my lifetime and have avoided getting my feet tangled in them. I've come across fixed-knot fences, post-and-rail fences, welded wire fences, and then some. No matter how many different fences I've seen, I have as many opinions about them. And if there's one thing I can still rely on, it's my opinion, so I'm bound to stick to it. I've seen it all, so I've come to the reasonable conclusion that I know it all. I know exactly what kind of fence I aim to avoid. Like the mule, my comfort zone is where the safety is. It's not a bad thing to know what I want, stand by it, and not let anyone sway me from my convictions. Stubbornness is not something easily grown out of either. We seniors are as stubborn as two-year-olds, who also admirably know exactly what they want and don't stop trying to get it. What have we got to lose? I've finally realized I can't change the world, but it requires me to change, adjust, adapt—and that's an impossible ask when I've been set in my ways for decades. Anyhow, I prefer the term *determined* rather than *stubborn*. But if you insist on calling me as stubborn as a mule, I'd rather take it as a compliment.

ON THE SELF-PENNED OBITUARY

I've lived a full life, so I'm leaning toward self-penning my obituary. After all, no one knows better than me how fast and furious I've lived. Facts are what we all want, right? See, my obituary will live on the internet well past my expiration date. So I want it to be a sizzling piece of online real estate, one that makes your head fall back as you laugh, one that shocks you to death (figuratively speaking), and one that'll stick in your mind long after I'm gone, like freshly spit bubble gum sticks to the bottom of a new pair of walking shoes, except not in the annoying sense. See, I've got a lot to say about life: the life I actually lived, the life I really wanted, and the life I foresee in the eternal afterlife. I intend for my obituary to entertain all of it. Space is unlikely to be a problem in an online obituary, since scrolling can literally go on forever, much like my soul. A little softening up the hard edges of my life won't hurt. Beefing up the scrawny parts of my existence will round out my obituary nicely. Sprinkling jokes here and there about the world in which I lived would give the boisterous folks I leave behind an opportunity to share a hoot. I fancy a little harmless embellishment too. I just wonder how much of it is legal. By the time it's published, I guess the legalities of the self-penned obituary wouldn't matter much to me. But once I'm done, I'll be remembered as a self-made billionaire who set an upward trajectory for the course of humankind and was admired as one of the most strikingly handsome men that ever lived. Please keep my actual photo out of it, just to keeps the facts straight, of course.

ON LIVING IN THE PAST

I feel my prospects of the future are rather dim, so I make the most of my time by reliving the past. And what a glorious past it was. I tell my wide-eyed grandkids stories of the adventures I've been privileged to have, like the time I sailed across the Atlantic and nearly made it to Pico Island before being attacked by one-eyed pirates. I bravely fought back along with hundreds of my shipmates. It was a harrowing battle, with thirty-six-inch swords clashing and fiery cannons bursting and the hard-won treasures of gold coins flying over the railings of the treacherously rocking ship and into the bottomless depths of the blue ocean—but I lived to tell the tale. Nothing makes the present more palatable than seeing the sparkle in my grandkids' eyes as I recount the wondrous escapades I've lived through. I can back up my stories too. I tell them my wooden cane is carved from the timber of my beloved ship, lost forever in a watery grave at the bottom of the ocean. I suddenly become a hero, worthy of some highest medallion of honor, and I feel fantastically satisfied. Frankly, upon reliving the audacious past I invent with the help of my vivid imagination, my days are never dull.

ON SENIOR DATING

Dating tends to be a little different once seniorhood rolls around. Whenever I go on a smoking-hot senior date with an attractive femme fatale in her floral-patterned adaptive dress, I always wear my GPS tracker. It's discreetly strapped to my wrist like a contemporary smartwatch, so I'm rarely embarrassed or inconvenienced. In fact, I tell my date it's a fitness device that provides health metrics, which it miraculously does. I never leave home without it, as I don't want to get lost and not return before the clock strives twelve—noon, that is. I don't venture far anyhow, and especially never to a location that's outside of a familiar ten-mile radius. To accommodate everyone's schedule, I arrange my dates for early lunchtime, just to be sure I'm back in time to catch my favorite afternoon 80s sitcom reruns before napping, having a light dinner, and hitting the sack promptly at eight o'clock. I keep my date happy by parking as close to the restaurant as possible, particularly in the handicapped parking when it's available; my handicapped parking sign simplifies life's challenges for both us, so it's essential I never forget it. Once inside the restaurant, I make it a point to not order the scanty senior meals, and I advise my date to do the same. My cane or walker is always kept conveniently close. All the extra effort involved in senior dating results in two very contented aging partners. I highly recommend my specialized dating regimen to anyone who wishes to experience the same.

ON GETTING BETTER WITH AGE

Not everything fresh and new in life is necessarily better, more appealing, or more desirable. Some of life's special indulgences, like gouda cheese, red wine, and seniordom, actually improve with age. Like flannel sheets regularly tossed into the wash, our smiles and skin soften over time, until our inviting hugs are perfectly warm and cuddly. New leather sofas are too stiff for ease until a good number of years have passed and the leather has had a chance to smooth out, like the ripples in a pond after skipping stones in the water; it's no wonder the wee folks turn to us for the remarkable coziness only we aging grandparents exude. Ever tried flipping an egg on a brand-new cast-iron skillet? It doesn't work that way. A new skillet lacks the seasoning built up over months of cooking and reseasoning, the same way our life experiences gradually accumulate, finally giving us an estimable degree of wisdom found in no other age group. So you see, like avocados plucked from the evergreen fruit tree, many of us get more earthy, though some of us slightly nuttier, with time.

ON BEING FOREVER YOUNG

Although we seniors chronologically belong to the same age group, some of us remain remarkably youthful in comparison to our peers. In fact, we've stalwartly remained young for nearly three-quarters of an entire century, and nothing short of that. While some of us are as stale as the uncirculated air in an unventilated master bedroom, others are as youthful as the fresh dew on a four-leaf clover. The young at heart make frequent social visits, like to the Elk Lodge at the edge of town, spreading good cheer to longtime friends as if it's contagious. We're free spirits until either our minds or bodies fail. Even then, don't try to hold us back; we've got every intention of squeezing out every drop of life left to us—and we'll do so as long as we possess the grip strength. But if it comes down to it, we'll spurn the manual two-in-one lemon juicer and resort to an electric lemon squeezer instead. Even the stubbornest of seniors can appreciate that technology makes squeezing lemons realistically possible again. So on the exterior, our appearances and mannerisms tell one story, but on the inside, you'll be privy to a dramatically different—and often fabulous—one. Freshly squeezed lemonade, anyone?

Thank you for reading *In Defense of Seniorhood*.
If you enjoyed this collection of humorous essays,
please consider leaving a review at your favorite retailer
and helping other readers discover charmingly
off-the-rocker books of humor.

Books in the In Defense Of series
In Defense of Babyhood
In Defense of the Grim Reaper
In Defense of Misfortune

Visit my author website
www.riyapresents.com

www.ingramcontent.com/pod-product-compliance
Lightning Source LLC
Chambersburg PA
CBHW070945120626
46546CB00004B/1566